ISTANBUL
TRAVEL GUIDE 2023-2024

Your In-Depth Companion to Unlocking the City's Hidden Gems, Uncovering Its Treasures, and Revealing Its Best-Kept Secrets

RICK EMMANUEL

No part of this publication may be reproduced, stored or transmitted in any form or by any means, electronic, mechanical, photocopying, recording, scanning, or otherwise without written permission from the publisher.

It is illegal to copy this book, post it to a website, or distribute it by any other means without permission.

**Copyright © 2024 Rick Emmanuel
All rights reserved.**

DISCLAIMER:

Take note that the information provided in this travel guide is subject to change and may not always be accurate or up-to-date.

While every effort has been made to ensure the information provided is reliable, we cannot be held responsible for any errors, omissions, or changes that may occur.

It is recommended that you verify any important information, such as entry requirements, travel restrictions, and local customs, with relevant authorities before embarking on your journey.

Additionally, please be aware that travelling can be inherently risky, and we cannot be held liable for any accidents, injuries, illnesses, or losses that may occur during your travels.

ISTANBUL

TABLE OF CONTENTS

INTRODUCTION
Istanbul: A City of Two Continents
A Brief History of Istanbul
Istanbul Today

ISTANBUL HIGHLIGHTS
Top 10 Things to Do in Istanbul
Top 10 Culinary Highlights in Istanbul
Top 10 Festivals and Events in Istanbul

SULTANAHMET AND THE OLD CITY
Hagia Sophia
Topkapi Palace
Blue Mosque
Archaeological Museums
Grand Bazaar
Hippodrome

OTHER NEIGHBORHOODS
Beyoğlu
Galata Tower
Istiklal Caddesi
Taksim Square
Spice Bazaar
Balat
Fener
Golden Horn
Bosphorus

SELF-DIRECTED TOURS AND WALKS
Old Town Tour
Golden Horn Walk
New District Walk
Bosphorus Cruise
Asian Istanbul Walks

ISTANBUL HIDDEN GEMS AND SECRETS
Hidden Gems of Istanbul
Uncovering Istanbul's Treasures

Revealing Istanbul's Best-Kept Secrets

BEYOND ISTANBUL
Ephesus
Cappadocia

PRACTICAL INFORMATION
Getting to and Around Istanbul
Accommodation
Food and Drink
Shopping
Currency and Exchange
LanguageTips for Travelers

APPENDIX
Climate
Survival Phrases
Packing Checklist

Tour through the city of ISTANBUL with ISTANBUL TRAVEL GUIDE 2023-2024, so you will have an unforgettable trip ever.

INTRODUCTION

Joshua's heart raced with excitement as he stepped off the plane and into the bustling city of Istanbul. He had been dreaming of visiting this vibrant metropolis for years, and now he was finally here.

He had purchased a copy of the Istanbul Travel Guide 2023-2024 : Your In-Depth Companion to Unlocking the City's Hidden Gems, Uncovering Its Treasures, and Revealing Its Best-Kept Secrets.

He had spent weeks studying it, eager to plan his perfect itinerary.

Joshua's first stop was the Hagia Sophia, a former church and mosque that is now a museum. He was awestruck by the stunning architecture and mosaics, which date back to the 6th century.

Next, he headed to the Topkapi Palace, the main residence of the Ottoman sultans for over 400 years.

He wandered through the lavishly decorated rooms and courtyards, marvelling at the opulence of the Ottoman Empire.

Joshua also visited the Blue Mosque, one of the largest and most beautiful mosques in the world.

He was impressed by the six minarets and the intricate blue tiles that adorn the interior walls.

In addition to the major tourist attractions, Joshua was also eager to explore Istanbul's hidden gems. He followed the advice of his travel guide and visited the Chora Church, a Byzantine church known for its well-preserved mosaics.

He also wandered through the narrow streets of the Balat and Fener neighbourhoods, admiring the colourful houses and historic churches and synagogues.

One of Joshua's favourite experiences was taking a Bosphorus cruise. He sailed past the city's many landmarks, including the Hagia Sophia, Topkapi Palace, and Blue Mosque.

He also enjoyed the views of the city skyline and the Golden Horn.

Joshua also spent time exploring Istanbul's culinary scene. He tried traditional Turkish dishes such as kebabs, baklava, and Turkish coffee.

He also visited the Grand Bazaar, one of the largest and oldest covered markets in the world. He bargained with shopkeepers for souvenirs and spices.

After a week in Istanbul, Joshua was sad to leave. He had fallen in love with the city's rich history, culture, and cuisine. He knew that he would be back someday.

As he boarded his flight home, Joshua reflected on his amazing experience in Istanbul.

He was grateful for his travel guide, which had helped him to unlock the city's hidden gems, uncover its treasures, and reveal its best-kept secrets.

Istanbul: A City of Two Continents

Istanbul is a truly unique city, straddling two continents and three seas. It is the largest city in Turkey and one of the most populous in the world.

Istanbul has a rich history, dating back over 2,500 years, and has been the capital of several empires, including the Roman, Byzantine, and Ottoman empires.

The city's unique location has made it a crossroads for trade and culture for centuries.

Today, Istanbul is a cosmopolitan metropolis with a vibrant economy and a diverse population.

It is also a major tourist destination, attracting visitors from all over the world to see its many historical and cultural attractions.

A Brief History of Istanbul

The site of modern-day Istanbul has been inhabited since the 7th century BC. In 667 BC, the Greek colonists founded the city of Byzantium, which would later become the capital of the Byzantine Empire.

The Byzantine Empire was one of the most powerful empires in the world for over a thousand years.

During this time, Constantinople (as Istanbul was then known) was a major centre of learning and culture.

It was also a key strategic location, controlling the trade routes between Europe and Asia.

In 1453, the Ottoman Empire conquered Constantinople, bringing an end to the Byzantine Empire. The Ottomans ruled Istanbul for over 400 years, during which time the city became one of the most important cities in the Muslim world.

The Ottoman Empire collapsed after World War I, and Istanbul became the capital of the newly formed Republic of Turkey in 1923.

Since then, Istanbul has undergone rapid modernization and development. It is now a major economic and cultural centre for Turkey and the region.

Istanbul Today

Istanbul is a vibrant and cosmopolitan city with a population of over 15 million people.

It is a major centre for business, finance, culture, and education. The city is also home to a number of international organisations, including the Organization for Islamic Cooperation and the Black Sea Economic Cooperation.

Istanbul is a popular tourist destination, attracting visitors from all over the world to see its many historical and cultural attractions. Some of the most popular tourist attractions in Istanbul include:

Hagia Sophia: A former church and mosque, which is now a museum.

Topkapi Palace: The former residence of the Ottoman sultans.

Blue Mosque: One of the largest and most beautiful mosques in the world.

Grand Bazaar: One of the oldest and largest covered markets in the world.

Spice Bazaar: A market selling spices, herbs, and other Turkish culinary delights.

Bosphorus Cruise: A boat trip on the Bosphorus Strait, which divides Istanbul into European and Asian sides.

Istanbul is also a great city for foodies. The city has a diverse culinary scene, with restaurants serving everything from traditional Turkish cuisine to international fare. Some of the most popular dishes to try in Istanbul include:

Kebab: Grilled meat skewers.

Baklava: A sweet pastry made with layers of phyllo dough, nuts, and honey.

Turkish coffee: A strong and flavorful coffee made with finely ground coffee beans.

Istanbul is a fascinating and vibrant city with something to offer everyone. Whether you are interested in history, culture, food, or simply want to experience a unique and exotic destination, Istanbul is the perfect place for you.

ISTANBUL HIGHLIGHTS

Welcome to the vibrant and culturally rich city of Istanbul! In this comprehensive guide, we'll take you on a journey through the top attractions, culinary delights, and exciting festivals and events that Istanbul has to offer in the years 2023-2024.

Whether you're a history enthusiast, a food lover, or someone looking for a memorable cultural experience, Istanbul has something for everyone.

Join us as we explore the must-visit places, savour mouthwatering Turkish cuisine, and immerse ourselves in the festivities that make Istanbul a truly enchanting destination.

Top 10 Things to Do in Istanbul

Hagia Sophia: This iconic building has been a church, a mosque, and a museum over the centuries.

It is known for its stunning architecture and mosaics.

Topkapi Palace: This former residence of the Ottoman sultans houses a vast collection of treasures, including jewellery, weapons, and clothing.

Blue Mosque: This beautiful mosque is one of the largest and most popular tourist attractions in Istanbul.

Grand Bazaar: This covered market is one of the oldest and largest in the world. It is a great place to shop for souvenirs and Turkish handicrafts.

Spice Bazaar: This market sells spices, herbs, and other Turkish culinary delights. It is a great place to experience the sights and smells of Istanbul.

Bosphorus Cruise: A boat trip on the Bosphorus Strait is a great way to see some of Istanbul's most iconic landmarks, such as the Hagia Sophia, Topkapi Palace, and the Blue Mosque.

Süleymaniye Mosque: This mosque was built by the Ottoman sultan Süleyman the Magnificent and is considered to be one of the finest examples of Ottoman architecture.

Chora Church: This Byzantine church is known for its well-preserved mosaics, which depict scenes from the Bible.

Galata Tower: This mediaeval tower offers stunning views of Istanbul.

Istiklal Caddesi: This pedestrian street is one of the most popular shopping and entertainment districts in Istanbul.

Top 10 Culinary Highlights in Istanbul

Kebab: Grilled meat skewers are a staple of Turkish cuisine and there are many different varieties to choose from, such as döner kebab, şiş kebab, and adana kebab.

Baklava: This sweet pastry is made with layers of phyllo dough, nuts, and honey. It is one of the most popular desserts in Turkey.

Turkish coffee: This strong and flavorful coffee is made with finely ground coffee beans and served in small cups.

Meze: Meze are small dishes that are served before the main meal. They are a great way to sample a variety of Turkish flavors.

Simit: This ring-shaped bread is encrusted with sesame seeds and is a popular breakfast or snack food.

Döner kebab: This type of kebab is made from meat that is cooked on a rotating spit and then sliced off and served in a pita bread with salad and vegetables.

Baklava ice cream: This unique dessert combines ice cream with baklava and is a must-try for any visitor to Istanbul.

Turkish delight: This sweet candy is made with starch and sugar and comes in different flavours, such as rose, lemon, and pistachio.

Ayran: This yoghourt drink is a popular accompaniment to meals.

Çay: Turkish tea is a light and refreshing tea that is served in small glasses.

Top 10 Festivals and Events in Istanbul

Istanbul Music Festival: This festival features performances by classical, jazz, and folk musicians from all over the world.

Istanbul Jazz Festival: This festival attracts some of the biggest names in jazz music.

Istanbul Biennial: This contemporary art festival takes place every two years and features works by artists from all over the world.

Istanbul Film Festival: This film festival showcases Turkish and international films.

Istanbul Tulip Festival: This festival celebrates the city's tulips, which bloom in abundance during the spring months.

Ramadan: The Islamic holy month of Ramadan is a special time to visit Istanbul, as the city's mosques and bazaars are decorated and there are many special events and activities taking place.

Eid al-Fitr: This festival marks the end of Ramadan and is celebrated with feasting and festivities.

Turkish Republic Day: This national holiday is celebrated on October 29th and features parades, fireworks, and other festivities.

New Year's Eve: Istanbul is a great place to celebrate New Year's Eve, with many events and parties taking place all over the city.

Istanbul Shopping Festival: This festival takes place in June and July and features discounts and promotions at many of the city's shops and malls.

As we conclude our exploration of Istanbul's highlights, both in terms of its captivating landmarks and its delectable culinary offerings, we hope you've gained valuable insights into this remarkable city.

Istanbul's blend of tradition and modernity, its rich history, and its warm hospitality make it a destination that leaves a lasting impression on all who visit. The city's festivals and events further add to its allure, offering unique opportunities to connect with the local culture.

SULTANAHMET AND THE OLD CITY

Sultanahmet is the historic centre of Istanbul, and is home to many of the city's most iconic landmarks, including the Hagia Sophia, Topkapi Palace, and the Blue Mosque.

This vibrant neighbourhood is also home to a maze of narrow streets, bustling bazaars, and traditional Turkish restaurants.

Hagia Sophia

The Hagia Sophia is one of the most iconic buildings in the world, and is a must-see for any visitor to Istanbul.

This former church and mosque is now a museum, and its stunning architecture and mosaics are a testament to its rich history.

The Hagia Sophia was built in the 6th century by the Byzantine emperor Justinian I. It was originally a church, but was converted into a mosque after the Ottoman conquest of Constantinople in 1453.

In the early 20th century, the Hagia Sophia was converted into a museum, and it is now one of the most popular tourist attractions in Istanbul.

Visitors to the Hagia Sophia can admire its stunning architecture, which includes a massive dome, towering columns, and intricate mosaics.

The mosaics depict scenes from the Bible and the life of the Virgin Mary, and are some of the finest examples of Byzantine art in the world.

Topkapi Palace

Topkapi Palace was the main residence of the Ottoman sultans for over 400 years.

It is now a museum, and houses a vast collection of Ottoman treasures, including jewellery, weapons, clothing, and religious relics.

Topkapi Palace is a sprawling complex of buildings and courtyards. Visitors can explore the harem, where the sultan's wives and concubines lived; the imperial treasury, where the sultan's jewels and other valuables were kept; and the kitchens, where meals were prepared for the sultan and his court.

Topkapi Palace is also home to a number of gardens, including the Privy Garden, where the sultan and his family could relax and enjoy the outdoors.

Blue Mosque

The Blue Mosque is one of the largest and most beautiful mosques in the world.

It was built in the 17th century by the Ottoman sultan Ahmed I, and is known for its six minarets and its interior walls, which are decorated with blue tiles.

The Blue Mosque is a working mosque, and is open to visitors outside of prayer times. Visitors can admire the mosque's stunning architecture and interior design, and learn about Islamic culture and traditions.

Archaeological Museums

The Archaeological Museums in Istanbul house a vast collection of artefacts from Turkey's rich history.

The museums include the Museum of the Ancient Orient, the Museum of Turkish and Islamic Arts, and the Museum of Archaeology.

The Museum of the Ancient Orient houses a collection of artefacts from Mesopotamia, Anatolia, and Syria.

The Museum of Turkish and Islamic Arts houses a collection of artefacts from the Ottoman Empire and other Islamic cultures. The Museum of Archaeology houses a collection of artefacts from Turkey's pre-Islamic history.

The Archaeological Museums are a must-see for any visitor to Istanbul who is interested in history and culture.

Grand Bazaar

The Grand Bazaar is one of the oldest and largest covered markets in the world. It is a maze of narrow streets and stalls selling everything from carpets and spices to jewelry and clothing.

The Grand Bazaar is a great place to shop for souvenirs and experience the sights and smells of Istanbul.

Visitors can bargain with shopkeepers for the best prices, and enjoy a cup of Turkish coffee or tea at one of the many cafes in the market.

Hippodrome

The Hippodrome was the center of public life in Constantinople for centuries. It was used for chariot races, horse races, and other public events.

Today, the Hippodrome is a public park, and is home to a number of historical monuments, including the Obelisk of Theodosius, the Serpentine Column, and the Column of Constantine.

The Hippodrome is a great place to relax and enjoy the outdoors. Visitors can also learn about the history of Constantinople and the Byzantine Empire by visiting the Hippodrome Museum.

Getting to Sultanahmet

Sultanahmet is located in the heart of Istanbul and is easily accessible by public transportation. The area is also served by a number of taxi and minibus companies.

Tips for Visiting Sultanahmet

- Sultanahmet is a popular tourist destination, so it is important to be prepared for crowds.
- Visitors should dress respectfully when visiting mosques and other religious sites.
- It is important to bargain when shopping at the Grand Bazaar and other markets.
- Visitors should be aware of their surroundings and take precautions to avoid pickpockets and other scams.

Sultanahmet and the Old City are a must-see for any visitor to Istanbul.

This vibrant neighbourhood is home to many of the city's most iconic landmarks, as well as a maze of narrow streets, bustling bazaars, and traditional Turkish restaurants.

OTHER NEIGHBORHOODS

Istanbul is a city of contrasts, and its many neighbourhoods offer visitors a glimpse into the city's rich history, culture, and diversity. From the bustling shopping streets of Beyoğlu to the traditional neighbourhoods of Balat and Fener, there is something for everyone in Istanbul.

In addition to the Sultanahmet and Old City, here are some of the other neighbourhoods in Istanbul that visitors should consider exploring:

Beyoğlu

Beyoğlu is a vibrant neighbourhood located on the European side of Istanbul. It is home to many of the city's most popular tourist attractions, including Taksim Square, Istiklal Caddesi, and Galata Tower. Beyoğlu is also a great place to shop, dine, and enjoy the nightlife.

Galata Tower

Galata Tower is a medieval tower that offers stunning views of Istanbul. It was built in the 14th century, and is one of the most popular tourist attractions in the city.

Visitors can take an elevator to the top of the tower for panoramic views of Istanbul, the Golden Horn, and the Bosphorus Strait.

Istiklal Caddesi

Istiklal Caddesi is a pedestrian street that is lined with shops, cafes, and restaurants. It is one of the most popular shopping streets in Istanbul, and is also a great place to people-watch.

Taksim Square

Taksim Square is the heart of Beyoğlu and is a popular gathering place for locals and tourists alike.

The square is home to a number of monuments, including the Republic Monument and the Atatürk Cultural Center. Taksim Square is also a great place to catch a bus or metro to other parts of the city.

Spice Bazaar

The Spice Bazaar is a covered market that sells spices, herbs, and other Turkish culinary delights. It is a great place to experience the sights and smells of Istanbul.

Visitors can bargain with shopkeepers for the best prices, and enjoy a cup of Turkish coffee or tea at one of the many cafes in the market.

Balat and Fener

Balat and Fener are two traditional neighbourhoods located on the Golden Horn.

These neighbourhoods are known for their colorful houses, narrow streets, and historic churches and synagogues. Balat and Fener are also home to a number of antique shops and art galleries.

Golden Horn

The Golden Horn is an inlet of the Bosphorus Strait that divides Istanbul into European and Asian sides. The Golden Horn is home to a number of historic landmarks, including the Süleymaniye Mosque, the Chora Church, and the Eyüp Sultan Mosque.

Visitors can take a boat cruise on the Golden Horn to see these landmarks and enjoy the views of the city.

Bosphorus

The Bosphorus Strait is a waterway that divides Istanbul into European and Asian sides.

It is one of the most important shipping routes in the world, and is also a popular tourist destination.

Visitors can take a boat cruise on the Bosphorus to see the city's many landmarks, including the Hagia Sophia, Topkapi Palace, and the Blue Mosque.

Istanbul is a city with something to offer everyone. Whether you are interested in history, culture, food, or shopping, you will find something to love in Istanbul.

The neighbourhoods listed above are just a few of the many places that visitors can explore in this vibrant city.

SELF-DIRECTED TOURS AND WALKS

Istanbul is a city with a rich history and culture, and there is no better way to experience it than on a self-directed tour or walk. With its many iconic landmarks and vibrant neighbourhoods, Istanbul has something to offer everyone.

Here are a few suggested self-directed tours and walks in Istanbul:

Old Town Tour

Start your tour at the Hagia Sophia, one of the most iconic buildings in the world. This former church and mosque is now a museum, and its stunning architecture and mosaics are a testament to its rich history.

Next, head to Topkapi Palace, the main residence of the Ottoman sultans for over 400 years.

This sprawling complex of buildings and courtyards houses a vast collection of Ottoman treasures, including jewelry, weapons, clothing, and religious relics.

After Topkapi Palace, visit the Blue Mosque, one of the largest and most beautiful mosques in the world.

This working mosque is open to visitors outside of prayer times, and visitors can admire its stunning architecture and interior design.

From the Blue Mosque, head to the Grand Bazaar, one of the oldest and largest covered markets in the world.

This maze of narrow streets and stalls sells everything from carpets and spices to jewellery and clothing. Be sure to bargain with shopkeepers for the best prices!

Golden Horn Walk

Start your walk at the Süleymaniye Mosque, one of the most magnificent mosques in Istanbul. This mosque was built by the Ottoman sultan Süleyman the Magnificent in the 16th century, and is considered to be one of the finest examples of Ottoman architecture.

From the Süleymaniye Mosque, walk down to the Golden Horn, an inlet of the Bosphorus Strait that divides Istanbul into European and Asian sides. Take a stroll along the waterfront and enjoy the views of the city skyline.

Next, visit the Chora Church, a Byzantine church that is known for its well-preserved mosaics.

These mosaics depict scenes from the Bible and the life of the Virgin Mary, and are some of the finest examples of Byzantine art in the world.

From the Chora Church, continue walking down the Golden Horn to the Eyüp Sultan Mosque, one of the most important Islamic pilgrimage sites in Istanbul.

This mosque is believed to be the burial place of Abu Ayyub al-Ansari, the standard bearer of the Prophet Muhammad.

New District Walk

Start your walk at Taksim Square, the heart of Beyoğlu and a popular gathering place for locals and tourists alike.

The square is home to a number of monuments, including the Republic Monument and the Atatürk Cultural Center.

From Taksim Square, walk down Istiklal Caddesi, a pedestrian street that is lined with shops, cafes, and restaurants.

This is one of the most popular shopping streets in Istanbul, and is also a great place to people-watch.

Next, visit the Galata Tower, a mediaeval tower that offers stunning views of Istanbul. It was built in the 14th century, and is one of the most popular tourist attractions in the city.

Visitors can take an elevator to the top of the tower for panoramic views of Istanbul, the Golden Horn, and the Bosphorus Strait.

Bosphorus Cruise

There is no better way to see Istanbul's many landmarks than on a Bosphorus cruise. These cruises typically last for about two hours, and take passengers past some of the city's most iconic sights, such as the Hagia Sophia, Topkapi Palace, and the Blue Mosque.

Passengers can also enjoy the views of the city's many waterfront mansions and palaces. Bosphorus cruises are a great way to learn about Istanbul's history and culture, and to get a feel for the city's unique atmosphere.

Asian Istanbul Walks

There are a number of different walks that visitors can take in Asian Istanbul. One popular walk is the Kadıköy-Üsküdar walk, which takes visitors past two of the most popular neighbourhoods on the Asian side of Istanbul.

Kadıköy is a vibrant and cosmopolitan neighbourhood with a mix of old and new. Visitors can explore the narrow streets and alleyways of the old town, or visit the modern Kadıköy Bazaar.

Üsküdar is a more traditional neighbourhood, and is home to a number of historic mosques and churches.

Visitors can also take a ferry from Üsküdar to the Maiden's Tower, a mediaeval tower located on a small island in the Bosphorus Strait.

Another popular walk on the Asian side of Istanbul is the Beylerbeyi Palace Walk. Beylerbeyi Palace was built in the 19th century by the Ottoman sultan Abdül

Here are a few tips for planning your self-directed tours and walks:

- Wear comfortable shoes, as you will be doing a lot of walking.
- Bring a map or GPS device to help you navigate your way around the city.
- Be sure to drink plenty of water, especially during the hot summer months.
- Be respectful of local customs and traditions.
- Have fun and enjoy the experience!

These are just a few examples of self-directed tours and walks in Istanbul. With its many iconic landmarks and vibrant neighbourhoods, Istanbul has something to offer everyone. I encourage you to explore the city at your own pace and discover all that it has to offer.

BEYOND ISTANBUL

Istanbul is a fascinating and vibrant city, but there is more to Turkey than just its largest metropolis. Beyond Istanbul, visitors can find ancient ruins, stunning natural landscapes, and charming villages.

Two of the most popular destinations beyond Istanbul are Ephesus and Cappadocia.

Ephesus

Ephesus is an ancient Greek city located on the western coast of Turkey. It was one of the most important cities in the Roman Empire, and was home to a number of impressive temples, theatres, and libraries.

Today, Ephesus is a UNESCO World Heritage Site, and is one of the most popular tourist destinations in Turkey.

Visitors to Ephesus can explore the ruins of the city's many temples, including the Temple of Artemis, one of the Seven Wonders of the Ancient World.

They can also visit the Library of Celsus, a two-story library that was once home to over 12,000 scrolls.

In addition to its temples and libraries, Ephesus is also home to a number of other impressive ruins, including the Great Theater, which could seat up to 25,000 people, and the Terrace Houses, which were once the homes of wealthy Ephesians.

Cappadocia

Cappadocia is a region in central Turkey known for its unique geological formations and cave dwellings. The region is home to a number of valleys, each with its own unique landscape.

Some of the most popular valleys in Cappadocia include the Ihlara Valley, the Göreme Valley, and the Love Valley.

Visitors to Cappadocia can go hiking, biking, or horseback riding through the valleys. They can also visit the region's many cave dwellings, some of which date back to the 4th century AD.

In addition to its cave dwellings, Cappadocia is also home to a number of rock-cut churches and monasteries.

Some of the most popular rock-cut churches in Cappadocia include the Göreme Open Air Museum, the Karanlık Kilise (Dark Church), and the Selime Katedrali (Selime Cathedral).

Ephesus and Cappadocia are two of the most popular tourist destinations in Turkey. Both destinations offer visitors a chance to experience the country's rich history and culture.

Ephesus is home to some of the most impressive ancient ruins in the world, while Cappadocia is known for its unique geological formations and cave dwellings.

If you are planning a trip to Turkey, I encourage you to consider visiting Ephesus and Cappadocia. These two destinations offer something for everyone, and are sure to leave a lasting impression.

ISTANBUL HIDDEN GEMS AND SECRETS

Istanbul is a city of many layers, with a rich history and culture that dates back thousands of years. Beyond the city's iconic landmarks, there are also a number of hidden gems that are waiting to be discovered.

This chapter will reveal some of Istanbul's best-kept secrets, from ancient ruins to charming neighbourhoods to lesser-known museums.

Whether you are a first-time visitor or a seasoned traveller, you are sure to find something new to explore in Istanbul.

Hidden Gems of Istanbul

The Chora Church: This Byzantine church is known for its well-preserved mosaics, which depict scenes from the Bible and the life of the Virgin Mary.

Balat and Fener: These two traditional neighbourhoods are located on the Golden Horn and are known for their colourful houses, narrow streets, and historic churches and synagogues.

The Süleymaniye Mosque Complex: This complex includes a mosque, a school, a hospital, and a caravanserai.

The mosque is one of the most magnificent in Istanbul and offers stunning views of the city.

The Golden Horn: This inlet of the Bosphorus Strait divides Istanbul into European and Asian sides.

The Golden Horn is home to a number of historic landmarks, including the Süleymaniye Mosque Complex, the Chora Church, and the Eyüp Sultan Mosque.

The Bosphorus: This waterway connects the Black Sea and the Mediterranean Sea and divides Istanbul into European and Asian sides.

Visitors can take a boat cruise on the Bosphorus to see the city's many landmarks and enjoy the views of the city skyline.

Uncovering Istanbul's Treasures

The Museum of Turkish and Islamic Arts: This museum houses a vast collection of artefacts from the Ottoman Empire and other Islamic cultures.

The Archaeological Museums: These museums house a vast collection of artefacts from Turkey's rich history, including the Museum of the Ancient Orient, the Museum of Turkish and Islamic Arts, and the Museum of Archaeology.

The Museum of Mosaics: This museum houses a collection of mosaics from the Byzantine and Ottoman periods.

The Istanbul Modern: This museum is dedicated to modern and contemporary art in Turkey.

The Pera Museum: This museum houses a collection of Turkish and international paintings, sculptures, and decorative arts.

Revealing Istanbul's Best-Kept Secrets

The Pierre Loti Hill: This hill offers stunning views of the Golden Horn and the Bosphorus Strait.

The Maiden's Tower: This mediaeval tower is located on a small island in the Bosphorus Strait and offers stunning views of the city skyline.

The Sümela Monastery: This Byzantine monastery is located on a cliffside in the Trabzon Province and is one of the most iconic landmarks in northeastern Turkey.

The Pamukkale Terraces: These white travertine terraces are located in the Denizli Province and are a UNESCO World Heritage Site.

The Cappadocia Hot Air Balloon Rides: Cappadocia is a region in central Turkey known for its unique geological formations and cave dwellings.

Visitors to Cappadocia can take a hot air balloon ride to see the region's stunning landscape from above.

These are just a few of the many hidden gems of Istanbul. With its rich history and culture, Istanbul has something to offer everyone.

I encourage you to explore the city at your own pace and discover all that it has to offer.

Istanbul is a city that never ceases to amaze. With its rich history, culture, and architecture, there is always something new to discover. Whether you are a first-time visitor or a seasoned traveller, I encourage you to explore the city's hidden gems.

From ancient ruins to charming neighbourhoods to lesser-known museums, Istanbul has something to offer everyone. I hope this chapter has inspired you to uncover the city's treasures and reveal its best-kept secrets.

PRACTICAL INFORMATION FOR ISTANBUL

Istanbul is a major international city, and there are a number of ways to get to and around the city. Once you are in Istanbul, you will find a wide range of accommodation options, restaurants, and shops. This chapter will provide you with all the practical information you need to plan your trip to Istanbul.

Getting to Istanbul

Istanbul is served by two international airports: Istanbul Airport (IST) and Sabiha Gökçen Airport (SAW). Both airports are located about an hour from the city centre.

There are a number of ways to get from the airport to the city centre, including taxi, bus, and metro.

Taxis are the most expensive option, but they are also the most convenient. Buses are the most affordable option, but they can be crowded and slow. The metro is a good middle-ground option, and it is relatively fast and affordable.

Getting Around Istanbul

Istanbul has a comprehensive public transportation system that includes buses, metros, trams, and ferries.

The public transportation system is a great way to get around the city, and it is relatively affordable.

If you are staying in the city center, you will likely be able to get around on foot or by public transportation.

However, if you are staying in a more suburban area, you may want to consider renting a car.

Accommodation

Istanbul has a wide range of accommodation options, from budget hostels to luxury hotels. The best area to stay in depends on your budget and interests.

If you are on a tight budget, you may want to consider staying in a hostel in the Sultanahmet district.

If you are looking for a more luxurious experience, you may want to consider staying in a hotel in the Beyoğlu district.

Food and Drink

Istanbul has a diverse culinary scene, with restaurants serving everything from traditional Turkish cuisine to international fare. Some of the most popular Turkish dishes include kebabs, baklava, and Turkish coffee.

If you are looking for a truly authentic Turkish dining experience, you should try one of the many restaurants in the Sultanahmet district.

If you are looking for something more international, you will find a wide range of restaurants in the Beyoğlu and Nişantaşı districts.

Shopping

Istanbul is a great place to shop for everything from souvenirs to high-end fashion.

The Grand Bazaar is one of the largest and oldest covered markets in the world, and it is a great place to find souvenirs and traditional Turkish crafts.

If you are looking for high-end fashion, you should visit the Nisantasi district.

This district is home to a number of international designer brands, as well as Turkish boutiques.

Currency and Exchange

The official currency of Turkey is the Turkish lira (TRY). You can exchange your currency for Turkish lira at banks, currency exchange bureaus, and hotels.

It is important to note that the Turkish lira is a volatile currency, and its value can fluctuate frequently. It is a good idea to check the exchange rate before you travel to Istanbul, and to exchange enough currency to cover your expenses.

Language

The official language of Turkey is Turkish. However, English is widely spoken in tourist areas, and you should be able to get by without speaking Turkish.

If you are planning on spending a lot of time in Istanbul, it is a good idea to learn a few basic Turkish phrases.

This will show that you are making an effort to communicate with the locals, and it will make your trip more enjoyable.

Tips for Travelers

Istanbul is a safe city, but it is always important to be aware of your surroundings and to take precautions against petty theft.

Be respectful of Turkish culture and customs. For example, dress modestly when visiting religious sites.

Bargain when shopping at markets and bazaars.

Be prepared for crowds, especially during the summer months.

Learn a few basic Turkish phrases.

I hope this chapter has provided you with the practical information you need to plan your trip to Istanbul. With its rich history, culture, and food, Istanbul is a city that has something to offer everyone. I hope you have a wonderful time!

APPENDIX

Istanbul is a beautiful city with a rich history and culture. However, it is important to be prepared for the climate, learn a few survival phrases, and pack the right items when visiting.

Climate

Istanbul has a Mediterranean climate, with hot, dry summers and mild, wet winters. The average temperature in the summer is around 25 degrees Celsius, and the average temperature in the winter is around 5 degrees Celsius.

The best time to visit Istanbul is during the spring (April-June) or fall (September-October) when the weather is mild and sunny.

Survival Phrases

Here are some useful survival phrases in Turkish:

- **Merhaba.** (Hello.)
- **Teşekkür ederim.** (Thank you.)
- **Lütfen.** (Please.)
- **Ne kadar?** (How much?)
- **İngilizce konuşuyor musunuz?** (Do you speak English?)
- **Yardım edin!** (Help!)
- **Polis!** (Police!)
- **Doktor!** (Doctor!)
- **Tuvalet nerede?** (Where is the bathroom?)
- **Çıkış nerede?** (Where is the exit?)
- **Sağol.** (You're welcome.)
- **Afiyet olsun.** (Enjoy your meal.)
- **Evet.** (Yes.)
- **Hayır.** (No.)
- **Bilmiyorum.** (I don't know.)
- **Anlamıyorum.** (I don't understand.)

- **Yavaşça konuşabilir misiniz?** (Can you speak slowly?)
- **Tekrarlayabilir misiniz?** (Can you repeat that?)

Packing Checklist

Here is a packing checklist for Istanbul:

- Clothes for all types of weather, including layers for the cooler months.Comfortable shoes for walking.
- A hat, sunglasses, and sunscreen.
- A swimsuit and towel if you are planning on swimming.
- A camera to capture all of your memories.
- A Turkish phrasebook or app.
- An adapter if you are not from a country that uses European electrical plugs.
- Money and credit cards.
- Any necessary medications.

By following these tips, you can be prepared for your trip to Istanbul and enjoy all that this vibrant city has to offer.

CONCLUSION

Istanbul is a city that has something to offer everyone. With its rich history and culture, its stunning architecture, and its vibrant food scene, it is no wonder that Istanbul is one of the most popular tourist destinations in the world.

If you are planning a trip to Istanbul, I encourage you to use the Istanbul Travel Guide 2023-2024.

This comprehensive guide will help you plan your trip, choose the right accommodation, and find the best places to eat and shop. It will also help you discover Istanbul's hidden gems and uncover its treasures.

Here are a few additional tips for planning your trip to Istanbul:

Istanbul is a large city, so it is important to plan your transportation in advance. The public transportation system is efficient and affordable, but it can be crowded during peak hours. Taxis are also readily available, but they can be expensive.

Istanbul is a Muslim-majority country, so it is important to be respectful of local customs and traditions.

For example, dress modestly when visiting religious sites and avoid public displays of affection.

Istanbul is a relatively safe city, but it is always important to be aware of your surroundings and to take precautions against petty theft.

Learn a few basic Turkish phrases. This will show that you are making an effort to communicate with the locals, and it will make your trip more enjoyable.

I hope this travel guide has been helpful. With its rich history, culture, and food, Istanbul is a city that will stay with you long after you leave. Have a wonderful trip!

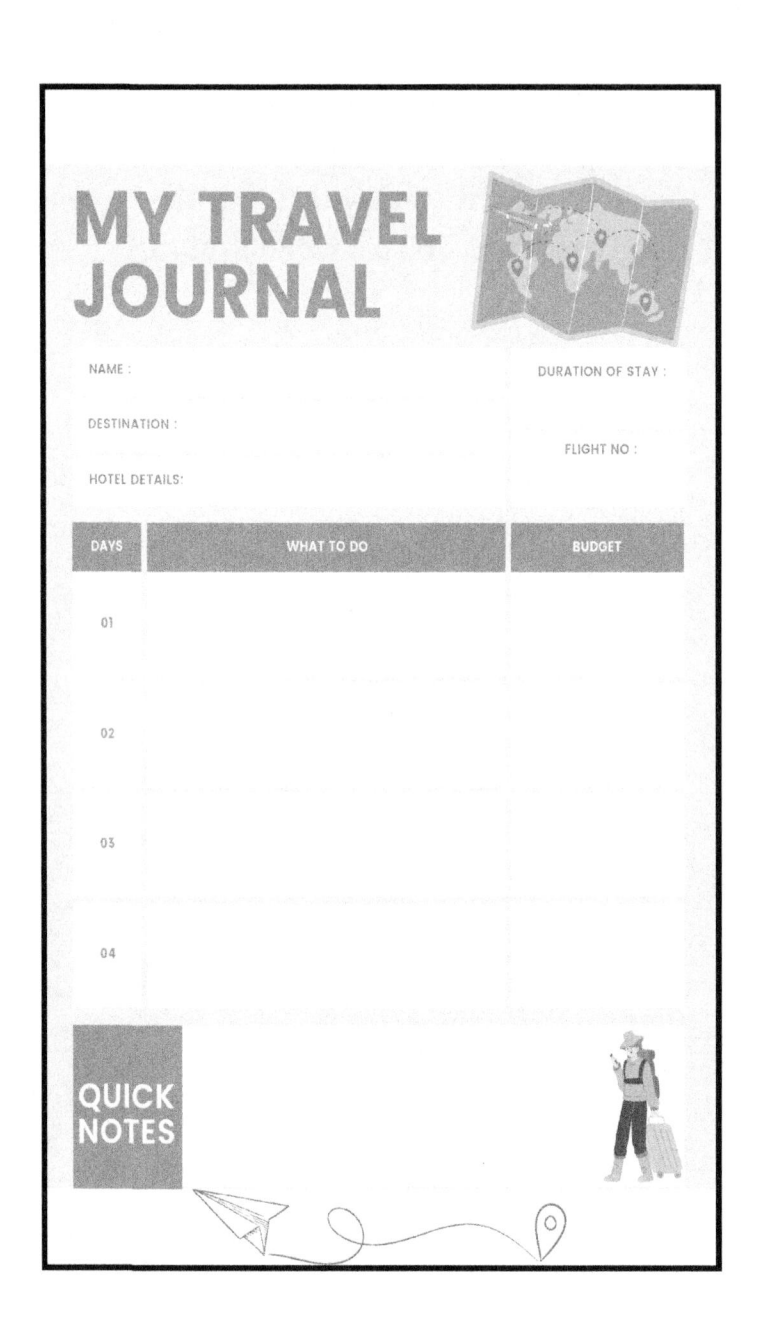

MY TRAVEL JOURNAL

NAME :

DURATION OF STAY :

DESTINATION :

FLIGHT NO :

HOTEL DETAILS:

DAYS	WHAT TO DO	BUDGET
01		
02		
03		
04		

QUICK NOTES

MY TRAVEL JOURNAL

NAME :

DURATION OF STAY :

DESTINATION :

FLIGHT NO :

HOTEL DETAILS:

DAYS	WHAT TO DO	BUDGET
01		
02		
03		
04		

QUICK NOTES

MY TRAVEL JOURNAL

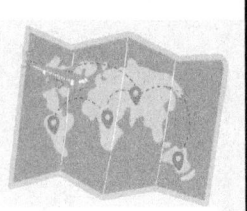

NAME :

DURATION OF STAY :

DESTINATION :

FLIGHT NO :

HOTEL DETAILS:

DAYS	WHAT TO DO	BUDGET
01		
02		
03		
04		

QUICK NOTES

MY TRAVEL JOURNAL

NAME :

DURATION OF STAY :

DESTINATION :

FLIGHT NO :

HOTEL DETAILS:

DAYS	WHAT TO DO	BUDGET
01		
02		
03		
04		

QUICK NOTES

THANK YOU!

Dear valued customers, if you enjoyed using our travel guides, we would be grateful if you could take just 5 seconds to leave a review.

Your feedback is highly appreciated and will help others make informed decisions about our products.

Thank you for choosing our travel guides and for your continued support.

Printed in Great Britain
by Amazon